Beyond Time and Space: A Love That Endures

Rajesh Giri

Published by Rajesh Giri, 2023.

BEYOND TIME AND SPACE: A LOVE THAT ENDURES

First edition. February 26, 2023.

Copyright © 2023 Rajesh Giri.

ISBN: 979-8215946244

Written by Rajesh Giri.

Table of Contents

Dedicated To

I am honored to dedicate this book to my beloved parents, the late Shri Kanti Giri and late Shrimati Champa Devi. They were not only my parents but also my greatest mentors and role models, who instilled in me a love of learning and a passion for seeking the truth.

Their unwavering support and encouragement throughout my life have been invaluable to me, and I will be forever grateful for their love and guidance. Although they are no longer with us, their legacy lives on through this book and my continued pursuit of knowledge and understanding.

I hope that this book serves as a fitting tribute to their memory and the profound impact they had on my life.

Legal Disclaimer

Copyright@Rajesh Kumar Giri - 2023

The information contained in the book **"Beyond Time and Space - A Love That Endures"** is for general guidance and educational purposes only. The author and publisher do not claim to offer any medical, legal, or financial advice, and readers should consult with a qualified professional before making any decisions based on the content of this book.

The author and publisher have made every effort to ensure the accuracy and completeness of the information provided in this book. However, they make no warranty or representation, express or implied, as to the accuracy or completeness of the information contained herein, and accept no responsibility for any errors or omissions.

The reader assumes all responsibility and risk for the use of the information contained in this book. The author and publisher shall have no liability whatsoever for any damages, including but not limited to direct, indirect, special, or consequential damages, arising out of or in connection with the use or inability to use the information contained in this book.

This book is not intended to be a substitute for professional advice, and the author and publisher strongly recommend that readers seek the advice of a qualified professional before making any decisions based on the information provided in this book.

Preface

Dear Reader,

Have you ever found yourself lost in a story, so captivated that you forget your own reality?

That's the power of a great book, and it's what we hope to accomplish with this one.

As Oscar Wilde once said, "It is what you read when you don't have to that determines what you will be when you can't help it." We believe that the stories we tell and the characters we create can have a profound impact on our lives, shaping who we are and who we become.

In the pages of this book, you'll find tales of love, loss, hope, and redemption, all woven together with a common thread: the human experience.

I have drawn inspiration from the words of Maya Angelou, who said, "I've learned that people will forget what you said, people will forget what you did, but people will never forget how you made them feel." Our hope is that these stories will make you feel deeply, connecting you to the characters and their journeys.

But as Stephen King reminds us, "The most important things are the hardest to say, because words diminish them." We know that our words can never fully capture the depth and complexity of the human experience, but we hope to come as close as we can.

Through these stories, we explore the many facets of what it means to be human: the joys and sorrows, the triumphs and failures, the love and the loss. I invite you to come along on this journey with us, to open your heart and your mind to the possibilities of the human experience.

As J.K. Rowling once wrote, "We do not need magic to transform our world. We carry all the power we need inside ourselves already." I believe that the power of storytelling can transform us, helping us to see the world in new and meaningful ways.

Thank you for embarking on this journey with me. I hope that these stories will leave a lasting impact on you, and that they will inspire you to continue exploring the many wonders of the human experience.
Sincerely,
Rajesh Kumar Giri

Beyond Time and Space

Love knows no bounds,
Transcending time and space,
A connection so profound,
Beyond any earthly place.

Beyond Time and Space: A Love That Endures is a heartwarming and inspiring book about the power of love to transcend the limitations of time and space. It is a book that tells the story of a couple whose love stood the test of time and distance, and whose bond remained strong even when faced with numerous challenges. The book is a tribute to enduring love and a celebration of the human spirit.

In today's fast-paced and transient world, relationships are often fragile and fleeting. Many people struggle to maintain a lasting connection with their loved ones, and often give up when faced with obstacles or setbacks. But there are some who refuse to give up on loves, who persevere through hardship and adversity, and who find a way to keep their bond alive despite the odds.

Beyond Time and Space: A Love That Endures is a book for those who believe in the power of love to conquer all obstacles. It is a book that explores the many facets of enduring love, from the challenges it faces to the joys it brings. Through the stories and experiences of real people who have lived and loved deeply, this book offers insights into the secrets of lasting love, and provides inspiration for anyone who seeks to build a strong and enduring relationship.

Chapter 1: The Beginning of an Enduring Love Story

"Every great love story starts with a simple moment, a fleeting glance, a chance encounter. But it's the commitment to love, the willingness to weather storms and stand the test of time, that transforms it into an enduring tale for the ages."

EVERY ENDURING LOVE story has a beginning; a moment when two hearts meet and a connection is made that transcends time and space. For many couples, this moment is one of chance or serendipity, a meeting that seems to happen by accident but is, in fact, the result of a higher plan. For others, it is the culmination of a long and arduous search, a moment of recognition when two souls finally find each other after a lifetime of waiting.

Whatever the circumstances, the beginning of an enduring love story is always marked by a sense of magic and wonder, a feeling that something special is unfolding. It is a time of excitement and anticipation, of getting to know each other and discovering the many ways in which two lives can intertwine. It is a time of shared dreams and hopes, of building a foundation for a future that is yet to come.

In this chapter, we will explore the beginnings of some real-life enduring love stories, and examine the elements that made them strong and enduring. We will see how chance encounters, mutual interests, and shared values all played a role in bringing these couples together, and how their love grew and deepened over time. We will also look at some of the challenges they faced in the early days of their relationship, and how they overcame them to build a bond that endured.

One such couple is Sarah and Michael, who met by chance at a coffee shop in New York City. Sarah was there to meet a friend, and Michael was there to grab a quick cup of coffee on his way to work. They struck up a conversation while waiting in line, and quickly discovered that they had a shared love of music and travel. They exchanged numbers and began dating, and soon found that they had an instant connection that felt both comfortable and exhilarating.

As their relationship grew, Sarah and Michael faced the challenge of distance, as Michael's job required him to travel frequently. They found ways to stay connected, however, through phone calls, text messages, and frequent visits when Michael was in town. They also made a point of sharing their travel experiences with each other, sending photos and souvenirs from their respective trips.

Another couple, Tom and Lisa, met through a mutual friend and quickly discovered that they had a shared passion for social justice and community service. They began volunteering together at a local shelter, and found that their work together deepened their connection and strengthened their bond. They also shared a love of the outdoors, and spent many weekends hiking and camping together.

As their relationship progressed, Tom and Lisa faced the challenge of blending their families, as both had children from previous relationships. They worked hard to create a harmonious and loving home, and found ways to make their blended family work through patience, understanding, and compromise.

These are just two examples of the many different paths that can lead to an enduring love story. What they all have in common, however, is a sense of shared purpose and mutual respect that forms the foundation of a strong and lasting relationship.

LET US RELAX WITH A romantic poem before exploring the next chapter

In the dawn of our love, a story began
Two hearts intertwined, destiny's plan
Through the twists and turns of fate
Our love grew stronger, never too late

A SPARK IGNITED, A flame grew bright
Passion and desire, day and night
Together we faced life's challenges and woes
Our love an anchor, through highs and lows

AS TIME PASSED, OUR love only grew
A bond unbreakable, forever true
Our story, an enduring tale of love
Written in the stars, guided from above

FROM THE BEGINNING, our hearts entwined
A love story for the ages, one of a kind
Through the ages, our love will endure
A flame that will never obscure.

IN THE NEXT CHAPTER, we will explore how love can transcend time and space, and how couples can maintain their connection even when they are physically apart.

Chapter 2: Love across Time and Space

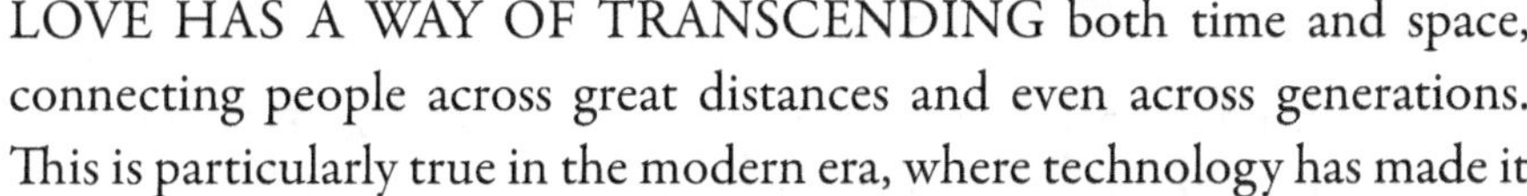

"Love across time and space transcends physical boundaries and defies the limits of our imagination. It is the bond that unites us, even when miles or centuries apart. Let us celebrate the enduring power of love that echoes through the ages, connecting hearts and souls in a cosmic dance of destiny."

LOVE HAS A WAY OF TRANSCENDING both time and space, connecting people across great distances and even across generations. This is particularly true in the modern era, where technology has made it easier than ever to stay connected with loved ones, no matter where they may be in the world.

One example of love across time and space is the story of Jane and John, who met while studying abroad in college. They fell deeply in love, but after graduation, John returned to his home country while Jane stayed in the United States. Despite the distance, they remained committed to their relationship, and found ways to stay connected through phone calls, video chats, and frequent visits.

Over time, their love only grew stronger, and they decided to get married. They faced the challenge of planning a wedding across an ocean, but with the help of family and friends, they were able to create a beautiful ceremony that brought together both of their cultures.

Another example of love across time and space is the story of James and Susan, who met later in life through an online dating site. They quickly discovered a shared love of travel and adventure, and began planning trips together to exotic locations around the world.

Despite the distance between them - James lived in the United States while Susan lived in Europe - they found ways to stay connected through frequent visits and constant communication. They also made a point of sharing their travel experiences with each other, sending photos and videos of their adventures.

Eventually, they decided to take the plunge and move in together, with James relocating to Europe to be with Susan. They faced the challenge of adjusting to a new country and culture, but with their shared love and commitment to each other, they were able to create a happy and fulfilling life together.

These stories demonstrate the power of love to transcend time and space, connecting people across great distances and even across cultures.

Activities that can help maintain a healthy relationship in Love across Time and Space:

1. Schedule regular video calls or phone calls to keep in touch and maintain a sense of connection.
2. Plan virtual dates together, such as watching a movie or cooking the same recipe while video chatting.
3. Send each other care packages with meaningful gifts or handwritten letters to keep the romance alive.
4. Write love letters to each other and mail them, creating a physical reminder of your love.
5. Play online games or engage in other shared activities, such as virtual book clubs or online workout classes.
6. Share your favorite songs, movies, and books with each other to find new ways to connect and deepen your bond.
7. Set goals together for your future as a couple and work towards them, even if you are physically apart.
8. Practice gratitude by expressing appreciation for each other and the relationship, even in small ways like saying "thank you"

or sending a quick text.

9. Take time to listen actively and empathetically to each other's concerns and feelings, even if they may be difficult to hear.
10. Remind each other of your commitment and dedication to the relationship, even when distance or other challenges arise.
11.

Let us check and read the love letter together - A real love letter written by the lover to his beloved.

My dearest Reshma,

As I sit down to write this letter, I am filled with longing for your presence. Even though miles separate us, our love is stronger than the distance that separates us.

"My love for you is as boundless as the ocean,

As timeless as the tides,

And as deep as the sea."

Every day, my heart aches to be near you, to feel your touch and to hear your voice. But until then, I will let my words carry my love across time and space to you.

I remember the day we met like it was yesterday. The way you smiled at me, the sound of your laughter, and the sparkle in your eyes - I knew I had found my soulmate. And now, as I look back on our journey together, I realize that our love has grown even stronger with each passing day.

"We may be separated by distance and time,

But our love knows no bounds,

And our hearts beat as one."

Through the trials and tribulations of life, our love has remained steadfast and true. I know that no matter where we are or what challenges we may face, our love will endure.

So, my beloved Reshma, I make this promise to you - to love you, to cherish you, and to hold you close, even across time and space.

Forever yours,

Badal

LET US RELAX WITH A romantic poem before exploring the next chapter

> Through the winds of time and space we travel,
> Our hearts entwined an unbreakable marvel.
> Distance fades as our love takes flight,
> Guiding us through darkness into the light.

ACROSS GALAXIES AND oceans deep,

> Our bond holds strong, true and sweet.
> With each passing day, our love does grow,
> Bound by fate, our passion does flow.

SO LET US CHERISH THIS love so rare,

> As we journey on without a care.
> For time and space may try to keep us apart,
> But nothing can ever break our heart.

IN THE NEXT CHAPTER, we will explore how couples can maintain their connection even during times of stress and adversity.

Chapter 3: Love in the Face of Adversity

"Love in the face of adversity is a flame that burns brighter and stronger than any challenge. It is the anchor that keeps us steady amidst the storm, and the light that guides us through the darkness. Let us embrace the power of love to conquer all obstacles, and emerge victorious in the face of adversity."

NO RELATIONSHIP IS without its challenges, and even the strongest couples will face times of stress and adversity. However, it is during these difficult moments that the true strength of a relationship is revealed, as couples work together to overcome obstacles and find a path forward.

One example of love in the face of adversity is the story of Maria and Miguel, who faced a difficult pregnancy when Maria was diagnosed with a high-risk condition. They worked together to manage the situation, with Miguel taking on extra responsibilities at work to ensure that he could be there to support Maria during doctor's appointments and other medical appointments.

When their baby was born prematurely, they faced even greater challenges, including a lengthy hospital stay and ongoing medical care. However, they remained committed to each other and to their family, finding strength in their love and support for each other.

Another example is the story of Alex and Rachel, who faced financial difficulties when Alex lost his job. They worked together to create a budget and find ways to make ends meet, with Rachel taking on extra shifts at work and Alex picking up odd jobs to make ends meet.

Despite the stress and uncertainty of their situation, they remained committed to each other, finding comfort and strength in their shared love and determination to overcome their challenges.

These stories illustrate the importance of resilience and commitment in the face of adversity, and the power of love to help us overcome even the most difficult situations.

Activities for couples to maintain a healthy relationship in the face of adversity:

1. **Practice open and honest communication:** When faced with adversity, it is important to communicate your feelings and concerns with your partner. This allows both of you to understand each other's perspective and work towards a solution together.

2. **Show support and empathy:** Be there for each other in difficult times and offer emotional support. Show empathy by acknowledging your partner's feelings and validating their experiences.

3. **Take care of yourselves:** In order to support each other, it's important to take care of yourself as well. Make sure to prioritize self-care activities such as exercise, healthy eating, and meditation.

4. **Plan enjoyable activities together:** While dealing with adversity can be tough, it's important to take time to enjoy each other's company and have fun together. Plan activities that you both enjoy and that bring you closer together.

5. **Seek professional help:** Sometimes, outside help is necessary to work through difficult times. Consider seeing a therapist or counselor together to help navigate any challenges you may be facing.

6.

Remember, no matter what challenges come your way, with love, support, and commitment, you can overcome anything together.

Tips for planning enjoyable activities together to sustain a healthy relationship in the face of adversity:

1. **Discuss interests:** Take time to understand each other's interests and find activities that you both enjoy. This will help ensure that the activities you plan are something you'll both look forward to.

2. **Get creative:** If your usual activities are limited due to adversity, try to get creative and find new activities to do together. This could be anything from cooking a new recipe together to trying a new hobby.

3. **Take turns planning:** Share the responsibility of planning activities and take turns choosing what to do. This will help keep things fresh and prevent one person from feeling overwhelmed.

4. **Keep it simple:** When dealing with adversity, it's important to remember that sometimes simple activities can be the most enjoyable. Don't feel like you have to plan elaborate outings or spend a lot of money to have fun together.

5. **Be flexible:** Remember that adversity can bring unexpected challenges, so it's important to be flexible with your plans. Don't get too attached to a specific activity or schedule, and be willing to adjust as needed.

Overall, the key is to find activities that bring you both joy and allow you to connect with each other. By planning enjoyable activities together, you can strengthen your relationship and face adversity as a team.

Let us relax with a romantic poem before exploring the next chapter

In the midst of stormy seas and crashing waves,
Our love stands firm, unwavering and brave.

Though trials may come and challenges arise,
Our hearts remain steadfast, never to compromise.

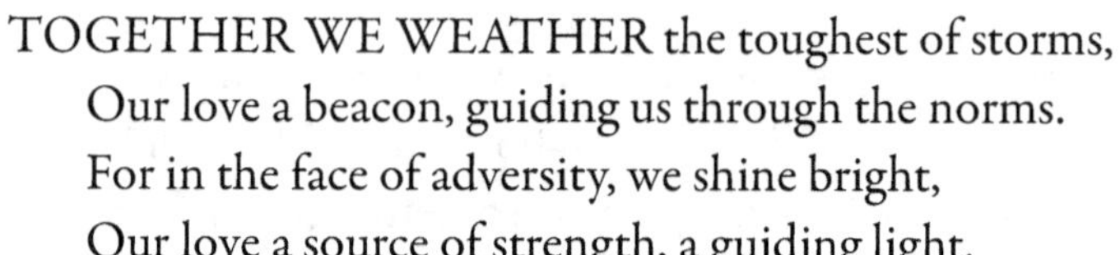

TOGETHER WE WEATHER the toughest of storms,
Our love a beacon, guiding us through the norms.
For in the face of adversity, we shine bright,
Our love a source of strength, a guiding light.

NO MATTER WHAT OBSTACLES come our ways,
Our love will endure, come what may.
For in the face of adversity, we stand tall,
Our love an unbreakable bond that conquers all.

IN THE NEXT CHAPTER, we will explore the role of communication in building strong and healthy relationships.

Chapter 4: The Importance of Communication in Relationships

"Communication is the bridge that connects two souls, allowing them to share their thoughts, dreams, and fears. It is the wind that carries the seeds of understanding, and the sun that illuminates the path to love. Let us cherish and practice open communication in our relationships, for it is the foundation on which all healthy connections are built."

EFFECTIVE COMMUNICATION is essential to building strong and healthy relationships. When couples are able to communicate openly and honestly, they are better able to understand each other's needs and work together to resolve conflicts and build a stronger connection.

One important aspect of communication is active listening. This means paying attention to what your partner is saying, and taking the time to understand their perspective. It also means being open to feedback and criticism, and using it as an opportunity to learn and grow together.

Another important aspect of communication is expressing your own needs and feelings in a clear and constructive way. This involves using "I" statements to express how you are feeling, rather than attacking or blaming your partner. It also involves being willing to compromise and work together to find solutions that meet both partners' needs.

Finally, it is important to establish clear boundaries and expectations in your relationship. This means being open and honest about what you are looking for in a relationship, and what you are willing to give in return. It also means being willing to set boundaries around things like time and space, and respecting your partner's boundaries as well.

Effective communication takes practice, and it requires a willingness to be vulnerable and open with your partner. However, when couples are able to communicate effectively, they are better able to build a strong and healthy relationship that can withstand the challenges and uncertainties of life.

Activities that can help improve communication in relationships:

1. **Daily check-ins:** Make it a habit to check in with your partner every day, even if it's just for a few minutes. Ask them how their day was and share your own experiences. This can help you stay connected and up-to-date on each other's lives.

2. **Schedule regular date nights:** Setting aside time each week or month for a special date night can create a safe space for open communication. Try to keep these dates technology-free to avoid distractions.

3. **Use active listening techniques:** Practice active listening by focusing on what your partner is saying without interrupting or getting defensive. Repeat back what you heard to ensure you understand their perspective.

4. **Take a communication workshop or course:** Enrolling in a workshop or course on communication can help you and your partner develop new skills and tools to better communicate with each other.

5. **Write each other letters:** Sometimes, it can be easier to express your thoughts and feelings in writing rather than in person. Consider writing letters to each other to communicate

important messages or express gratitude.

6. **Play communication games:** There are many games designed to improve communication skills, such as "The Ungame" or "Conversation Cubes". These can be fun and lighthearted ways to practice communicating effectively with your partner.

Remember that communication is key to any healthy relationship, so don't be afraid to try new methods to improve your communication skills.

Let us see and read the letter of a lover to her beloved to express thoughts and feelings in written rather than in person –

My Dearest Reshma,

The warmth of your love has ignited my heart and soul, and I can't imagine my life without you. I treasure every moment we spend together, and I'm grateful for the love we share. However, I feel that something is amiss between us, and I believe it's our communication.

The distance between us may be long,

But my love for you remains strong.

In every moment, in every thought,

It is your love that I have sought.

As we navigate this journey of love,

I am reminded of the importance of communication like a dove.

It is the foundation, upon which our love is built,

And the key to keeping our hearts fulfilled.

Let us take the time to talk and listen,

To express ourselves without any inhibition.

Let us share our thoughts, our dreams, our fears,

And through open communication, wipe away any tears.

In the face of any obstacle or strife,

Our love will thrive with strong communication in life.

So my love let us make a promise today,

To always communicate and never stray.

In any relationship, communication is key. I believe that we need to have open and honest communication to understand each other's thoughts, emotions, and needs. We should be able to share our feelings without fear of judgment or rejection.

AS RUMI ONCE SAID, "Silence is the language of love, let your words speak for you." So, I'm writing this letter to express my thoughts and feelings in writing rather than in person. I hope it will help us to communicate more effectively and strengthen our bond.

I WOULD LOVE FOR US to take some time out to talk about our day, share our achievements and frustrations, and listen to each other's perspectives. We can make it a daily ritual, maybe over a cup of coffee or a walk in the park.

I BELIEVE THAT OUR conversations will bring us closer and help us to build a more robust and enduring relationship.

Let's make a commitment to communicate more effectively, to be open and honest, and to listen with our hearts. Together, we can overcome any obstacle, and our love will continue to grow stronger with each passing day.

YOURS ALWAYS AND FOREVER,
   Badal

LET US RELAX WITH A romantic poem before exploring the next chapter

When words become the bridge that joins us,
Our love transcends the boundaries of trust,
As we share our thoughts and deepest desires,
Our bond grows stronger with each phrase we inspire.

THROUGH HEARTFELT CONVERSATIONS, we heal,
And bring light to the shadows we feel,
Our love blossoms with every spoken word,
And a love that lasts, forever shall be preserved.

IN MOMENTS OF SILENCE, we learn to listen,
To understand and show compassion,
With communication as our foundation,
Our love is strengthened with each conversation.

IN EVERY WORD, WE FIND solace and peace,
As we nurture a love that will never cease,
For in the power of communication,
Our love flourishes with sweet elation.

IN THE NEXT CHAPTER, we will explore the role of trust in building strong and healthy relationships.

Chapter 5: The Importance of Trust in Relationships

"Trust is the glue that binds two hearts together, creating a bond that is unbreakable and enduring. It is the foundation upon which all healthy relationships are built, and the seed from which love grows. Let us value and honor the trust in our relationships, for it is the key to unlocking a love that is pure and true."

TRUST IS THE FOUNDATION of any healthy and strong relationship. When couples trust each other, they are able to be vulnerable and open with each other, and build a deep sense of intimacy and connection.

There are several key components to building and maintaining trust in a relationship. The first is honesty. When couples are honest with each other, even about difficult or uncomfortable topics, they build a foundation of trust that can withstand challenges and difficulties.

Another key component is reliability. When couples are able to rely on each other to follow through on commitments and promises, they build a sense of trust and dependability that can deepen their connection.

Finally, it is important to be transparent and open with each other. This means sharing information and being willing to be vulnerable, even if it feels uncomfortable or difficult. It also means being willing to apologize and make amends when mistakes are made.

Trust takes time to build, but it can be easily broken if it is not nurtured and protected. It is important for couples to be mindful of their actions and words, and to work together to maintain the trust that they have built.

Understand the fact reading real story of couple from India

Reshma and Badal had been in a long-distance relationship for over a year. They had met through a mutual friend and had immediately hit it off. Even though they were miles apart, they talked to each other every day, sharing their hopes, dreams, and fears.

One day, Badal received a job offer that required him to move to another city. Reshma was happy for him, but also worried about what this meant for their relationship. She had heard stories of long-distance relationships falling apart due to lack of trust.

But Badal reassured her, telling her that he loved her and would do whatever it takes to make their relationship work. They made a plan to visit each other every few months and set aside time every day to talk to each other.

Over the next few months, they both went through ups and downs in their personal and professional lives. But through it all, they never stopped trusting each other. They were always honest and transparent about their feelings and were there to support each other in good times and bad.

Their relationship continued to grow stronger, and they knew that the foundation of their love was built on trust. They eventually got married and moved in together, but the importance of trust remained a central theme in their relationship.

Looking back, they realized that trust was not just important in long-distance relationships but in all relationships. It was the glue that held them together and made their love enduring.

Activities that can help build and strengthen trust in a relationship:

1. Have open and honest conversations about your expectations and boundaries in the relationship.
2. Take responsibility for your actions and follow through on your commitments.
3. Practice active listening to understand your partner's perspective and feelings.
4. Build intimacy through vulnerability and sharing personal experiences and emotions.
5. Show appreciation and gratitude for your partner's positive qualities and actions.
6. Spend quality time together, engaging in activities that both of you enjoy.
7. Apologize and make amends when mistakes are made, and forgive each other for past hurts.
8. Build mutual respect by valuing each other's opinions, feelings, and choices.
9. Practice empathy by putting yourself in your partner's shoes and understanding their experiences.
10. Be consistent in your actions and words to build a sense of reliability and dependability in the relationship.

Let us relax with a romantic poem before exploring the next chapter

In love, we seek a bond so true and strong,
Built on a trust that lasts a lifetime long,
A precious gem, the foundation of our hearts,
That shines through every trial and never departs.

WITH TRUST, WE OPEN up and freely give,

Our hopes, our dreams, and all we dare to live,
It's what makes love grow deep and take root,
A promise to hold steadfast and resolute.

FOR WHEN WE TRUST, we feel secure and free,
To be ourselves and love unconditionally,
And with each passing moment, we come to see,
The beauty of trust in all its majesty.

SO LET US HOLD OUR hearts and trust with care,
For in doing so, our love we truly share,
And let our love be the light that guides our way,
Through every challenge and each new day.

IN THE NEXT CHAPTER, we will explore the importance of intimacy and connection in building strong and healthy relationships.

Chapter 6: The Importance of Intimacy and Connection

"Intimacy and connection are the threads that weave together the fabric of our relationships, creating a tapestry that is both beautiful and strong. They are the nourishment that feeds the roots of our love, and the sunlight that helps it grow. Let us cherish and nurture intimacy and connection in our relationships, for they are the foundation on which all meaningful and lasting connections are built."

INTIMACY AND CONNECTION are essential components of any healthy and strong relationship. When couples are able to build intimacy and connection, they are able to deepen their emotional bond and create a sense of closeness that can withstand challenges and difficulties.

There are several ways to build intimacy and connection in a relationship. The first is through physical touch and affection. This includes things like holding hands, hugging, and kissing, and can help to create a sense of closeness and connection between partners.

Another way to build intimacy and connection is through emotional sharing and vulnerability. This means being open and honest about your feelings and experiences, and being willing to listen and support your partner in the same way.

It is also important to make time for each other, and to prioritize your relationship. This means setting aside time to spend together, whether it is going on a date, taking a walk, or simply spending time at home. It also means being willing to make compromises and sacrifices in order to prioritize your relationship.

Finally, building intimacy and connection also means being willing to work through challenges and difficulties together. This means being willing to listen to each other's perspectives, and to work together to find solutions that meet both partners' needs.

Building intimacy and connection takes time and effort, but it is essential to building a strong and healthy relationship.

Activities for building intimacy and connection in a relationship:

1. **Plan a surprise date night:** Surprise your partner with a special night out, such as a romantic dinner, a movie night, or a fun activity that you both enjoy.
2. **Write love letters to each other:** Take some time to write thoughtful and heartfelt letters to express your love and appreciation for each other.
3. **Take a couples' retreat:** Plan a weekend getaway to a beautiful location where you can disconnect from the world and focus on each other.
4. **Have a game night:** Play board games or card games together to have some lighthearted fun and laughter.
5. **Cook a meal together:** Plan a special meal and prepare it together, taking turns with the cooking and enjoying the final product.
6. **Share your hopes and dreams:** Take some time to share your deepest hopes and dreams with each other, and listen actively to your partner as they share theirs.
7. **Do a couples' activity:** Find an activity that you both enjoy, such as hiking, dancing, or painting, and do it together on a regular basis to build a deeper connection.
8. **Have a technology-free day:** Turn off your phones and other devices and spend the day together, focusing on each other and

building a stronger emotional connection.

Remember, building intimacy and connection takes time and effort, but the benefits to your relationship are immeasurable.

Let us relax with a romantic poem before exploring the next chapter

Intimacy and Connection, oh how sweet,
A bond between two hearts that cannot be beat,
A closeness that fills every single space,
A love that cannot be replaced.

HOLDING HANDS AND SOFT caresses,
Whispers of love, sweet and endless,
Looking into each other's eyes,
Feeling the world slowly die.

IN EACH OTHER'S ARMS, hearts beat as one,
Love and passion that cannot be undone,
Intimacy and Connection, a bond so true,
A love story that will forever renew.

IN THE NEXT CHAPTER, we will explore the importance of empathy and compassion in relationships.

Chapter 7: The Importance of Empathy and Compassion

"Empathy and compassion are the wings that allow our hearts to soar, and our love to reach new heights. They are the qualities that enable us to see the world through our partner's eyes, and to feel their joys and pains as if they were our own. Let us cultivate and nourish empathy and compassion in our relationships, for they are the seeds that bloom into a love that is boundless and profound."

Empathy and compassion are essential components of any healthy and strong relationship. When couples are able to practice empathy and compassion, they are able to deepen their emotional bond and create a sense of understanding and support that can withstand challenges and difficulties.

Empathy is the ability to understand and share the feelings of another person. When couples are able to practice empathy, they are able to better understand each other's perspectives and experiences, which can help to build a sense of connection and closeness.

Compassion, on the other hand, is the ability to show kindness and understanding to others, even when they are struggling or facing difficulties. When couples are able to practice compassion, they are able to support each other through challenging times and build a sense of trust and dependability in their relationship.

There are several ways to practice empathy and compassion in a relationship. The first is through active listening. This means being fully present and engaged when your partner is speaking, and taking the time to truly understand their perspective and feelings.

Another way to practice empathy and compassion is through validation. This means acknowledging and accepting your partner's feelings, even if you may not fully understand them. It also means being willing to offer support and encouragement when your partner is struggling.

Finally, it is important to practice empathy and compassion towards yourself as well. This means being kind and understanding towards yourself, even when you are facing challenges or difficulties.

Practicing empathy and compassion takes time and effort, but it is essential to building a strong and healthy relationship.

Activities for cultivating empathy and compassion in relationships:

1. **Practice active listening:** Make it a habit to really listen to your partner without interrupting or trying to solve their problems. This will help you understand their perspective and demonstrate your empathy towards their feelings.

2. **Put yourself in each-other shoes:** When your partner is going through a difficult time, try to imagine how you would feel if you were in such situation. This will help you better understand each-others emotions and show your compassion towards in struggles.

3. **Do something kind:** Small acts of kindness can go a long way in building a strong and compassionate relationship. Surprise your partner with a thoughtful gesture like making them breakfast in bed or leaving them a sweet note.

4. **Volunteer together:** Volunteering for a cause you both care about can be a great way to cultivate empathy and compassion together. It allows you to connect with each other and with those in need, while also fostering a sense of gratitude for what you have.

5. **Practice forgiveness:** Forgiving your partner for their mistakes can be a powerful way to demonstrate your empathy and compassion towards them. It shows that you are willing to let go of resentment and work towards a stronger relationship.

Let us relax with a romantic poem before exploring the next chapter

Softly spoken words,
Gentle touch of the hand,
A heart that's truly heard,
Together we'll stand.

IN TIMES OF NEED AND strife,
Empathy guides our way,
Compassion leads our life,
Love is here to stay.

WE UNDERSTAND EACH other,
In ways that words cannot express,
Our bond is like no other,
Our love is endless.

Chapter 8: The Role of Communication in Relationships

"Communication is the bridge that connects two hearts and minds, enabling us to share our thoughts, feelings, and experiences with each other. It is the foundation on which all relationships are built, and the key that unlocks the door to understanding and empathy. Let us never forget the power of communication in our journey towards deeper and more meaningful connections."

COMMUNICATION IS THE key to any successful relationship. Whether it's a romantic relationship, a friendship, or a professional one, effective communication can help build trust, strengthen connections, and solve problems.

In this chapter, we will explore the various aspects of communication in relationships, including the different types of communication, the barriers to communication, and how to improve communication for a more fulfilling and satisfying relationship.

Types of Communication:

Communication can take many forms, including verbal, nonverbal, and written. Verbal communication involves the use of words and can be either spoken or written. Nonverbal communication includes gestures, body language, and facial expressions. Written communication can include emails, text messages, and letters. Understanding the different types of communication and how they are used can help couples communicate more effectively.

Barriers to Communication:

There are several barriers to effective communication in relationships, including lack of trust, fear of conflict, and past experiences. It's important to identify these barriers and work to overcome them in order to have open and honest communication with your partner. Other barriers to communication can include misunderstandings, differences in communication styles, and cultural differences.

Improving Communication:

Improving communication in a relationship takes effort and practice. Some ways to improve communication include active listening, expressing emotions, and being open-minded. It's important to be respectful and non-judgmental when communicating with your partner, and to take the time to understand their point of view. Practicing effective communication can help build trust, strengthen connections, and solve problems in a relationship.

Conclusion:

Effective communication is essential to a healthy and successful relationship. Understanding the different types of communication, identifying barriers to communication, and working to improve communication can help couples build trust, strengthen connections, and resolve conflicts. By practicing good communication skills, couples can create a deeper and more meaningful relationship that will stand the test of time.

Activities for the role of communication in relationships:

1. **Take turns sharing your thoughts and feelings:** Set aside some time to talk to each other, and take turns sharing what's on your mind. Make sure you're actively listening to each other and asking questions to gain a better understanding.
2. **Play the "20 Questions" game:** Take turns asking each other

20 questions about anything and everything. This game can help you learn more about each other and deepen your connection.

3. **Write each other love letters:** Take the time to write a heartfelt letter to your partner expressing your love and appreciation for them. You can exchange the letters in person or leave them for each other to find.

4. **Watch a movie or TV show together and discuss it:** Choose a movie or TV show that interests both of you and watch it together. Afterward, discuss what you liked and didn't like about it and share your thoughts and opinions.

5. **Have a weekly check-in:** Set aside some time each week to check in with each other and discuss any issues or concerns you have. This can help prevent misunderstandings and ensure that you're both on the same page.

6. **Take a communication skills class:** Look for classes or workshops that focus on improving communication skills in relationships. This can help you learn new techniques for effective communication and deepen your connection with your partner.

7. **Play the "Mirror Game":** Sit facing each other and take turns mirroring each other's movements and expressions. This game can help you learn to communicate nonverbally and build a stronger emotional connection.

8. **Practice active listening:** When your partner is speaking, focus on actively listening and responding to what they're saying. Try to avoid interrupting or getting defensive, and instead focus on understanding their perspective.

9. **Take a social media break together:** Spend a day or weekend away from social media and other distractions. Use this time to focus on each other and engage in meaningful conversations and activities.

10. **Attend couples therapy:** If you're struggling with communication in your relationship, consider attending couples therapy. A therapist can help you learn new communication skills and work through any issues or conflicts.

LET US RELAX WITH A romantic poem before exploring the next chapter

The words we speak, the things we share,
Can make or break what we hold dear.
In love, in life, it's always there,
The need for open, honest care.

WE MUST EXPRESS, WE must confess,
Our thoughts and feelings, nothing less.
For when we talk, we can progress,
And heal the wounds that we suppress.

SO LET US LISTEN, LET us speak,
Let love and trust be what we seek.
In communication, we can find,
A deeper love, that's intertwined.

IN THE NEXT CHAPTER, we will explore the importance of trust and honesty in relationships.

Chapter 9: The Importance of Trust and Honesty

"Trust and honesty are the building blocks of strong and authentic relationships. They are the cornerstones that create a safe and secure space for us to be our true selves. Let us never take for granted the power of trust and honesty, for they are the hallmarks of a love that is both genuine and enduring."

TRUST AND HONESTY ARE two essential components of any healthy and strong relationship. When couples are able to trust each other and be honest with each other, they are able to build a strong foundation of respect and mutual understanding that can withstand challenges and difficulties.

Trust is the belief that your partner will be there for you, support you, and act in your best interest. When couples are able to trust each other, they are able to feel secure and confident in their relationship.

Honesty, on the other hand, is the willingness to be open and truthful with your partner, even when it may be difficult. When couples are able to be honest with each other, they are able to build a sense of transparency and authenticity in their relationship.

There are several ways to build trust and honesty in a relationship. The first is to be reliable and consistent. This means following through on commitments and being dependable in your actions and words.

Another way to build trust and honesty is to be open and transparent with your partner. This means being willing to share your thoughts, feelings, and experiences, even when they may be difficult or uncomfortable.

It is also important to be willing to listen and validate your partner's concerns and feelings. This means being open to feedback and criticism, and being willing to work together to find solutions to any issues or challenges that arise in the relationship.

Finally, it is important to be willing to forgive and move forward after mistakes or misunderstandings. This means being willing to apologize when necessary, and being willing to work together to rebuild trust and honesty in the relationship.

Building trust and honesty takes time and effort, but it is essential to building a strong and healthy relationship.

Activities for the Importance of Trust and Honesty in Relationships:

1. **Trust exercise:** Blindfold one person and have the other guide them around a room or outside area. This exercise helps build trust and communication between partners.
2. **Honesty game:** Play a game where partners take turns asking each other honest questions and answering them truthfully. This helps build a foundation of honesty in the relationship.
3. **Share secrets:** Take turns sharing personal secrets or fears with each other, and practice active listening and empathy towards your partner's feelings.
4. **Keep promises:** Make promises to each other, whether it's small things like making dinner plans or bigger commitments like saving up for a trip. Follow through on these promises to build trust and reliability.
5. **Appreciation notes:** Leave small notes or messages for your partner expressing your appreciation for them and their actions. This helps build trust and strengthens the bond

between partners.

6. **Conflict resolution:** Practice healthy conflict resolution by taking turns expressing your feelings and listening to your partner's perspective without interrupting or getting defensive. Find a solution together that works for both partners.

7. **Communication check-ins:** Set aside times each week to check in with each other and discuss any issues or concerns. This helps build open and honest communication in the relationship.

Remember that building trust and honesty takes time and effort, but it's worth it in the end for a strong and healthy relationship.

Let us relax with a romantic poem before exploring the next chapter

In your eyes, I find a truth so pure,
A trust that's deep and will endure.
Honesty, the cornerstone of our love,
A bond that's true and sent from above.

WITH EVERY WORD, WE build our trust,
A foundation strong, unbreakable and just.
We share our souls, with no pretense,
Our honesty, a gift that makes sense.

TOGETHER, WE HOLD EACH other's hearts,
A bond so pure, it never departs.
With trust and honesty, our love soars,
A connection strong, forevermore.

IN THE NEXT CHAPTER, we will explore the importance of intimacy and connection in relationships.

Chapter 10: The Power of Intimacy and Connection

"Intimacy and connection are the soulful threads that weave together the fabric of our relationships. They are the heartbeats that keep us in tune with each other's deepest desires and emotions. Let us cherish and nurture these sacred bonds, for they are the foundation of a love that is both passionate and profound."

INTIMACY AND CONNECTION are the foundations of any healthy relationship. It is the glue that binds two people together, enabling them to share their lives, feelings, and thoughts. Without intimacy and connection, a relationship can easily crumble under the weight of misunderstandings and conflicts.

In this chapter, we will explore the power of intimacy and connection in relationships and discover some activities that can help you deepen your connection with your partner.

Understanding the Importance of Intimacy and Connection

Intimacy and connection are not just physical; they are emotional, mental, and spiritual as well. It is the feeling of being close and connected to your partner, sharing your deepest thoughts and feelings without fear of judgment or rejection. When there is a deep sense of intimacy and connection, couples feel safe, secure, and supported, this allows them to tackle life's challenges together.

Benefits of Strong Intimacy and Connection

When couples prioritize intimacy and connection, they can experience several benefits, including:

1. Increased emotional support and understanding
2. Stronger bonds and a deeper sense of commitment
3. Improved communication and problem-solving skills
4. Enhanced sexual satisfaction and intimacy
5. Greater overall relationship satisfaction and happiness.

In conclusion, the power of intimacy and connection in relationships cannot be overstated. It is the key to building a strong and healthy relationship that can withstand the challenges of life.

By practicing the activities mentioned below and prioritizing intimacy and connection in your relationship, you can strengthen your bond with your partner and create a lasting, fulfilling partnership.

Activities for the power of intimacy and connection in relationships:

1. **Plan a date night:** Schedule a regular date night with your partner to spend quality time together. Choose activities that allow you to connect and be intimate, such as cooking a meal together, taking a dance class, or going on a romantic walk.
2. **Practice active listening:** Set aside time each day to listen to your partner without distractions. Use active listening techniques such as paraphrasing, clarifying, and summarizing to show that you understand and value their thoughts and feelings.
3. **Share your dreams and aspirations:** Take the time to share your hopes and dreams with your partner, and listen to theirs in return. This can help you build a deeper connection and understanding of each other's goals and desires.
4. **Create intimacy through touch:** Physical touch is an important way to build intimacy in a relationship. Make time

for regular cuddling, holding hands, and other forms of affectionate touch.

5. **Write love letters:** Take the time to write a heartfelt letter to your partner expressing your love and appreciation for them. This can be a powerful way to build intimacy and connection.

6. **Take a trip together:** Plan a romantic getaway or a weekend trip with your partner. This can be a great way to escape the stresses of daily life and focus on each other.

7. **Attend a couples' retreat:** Consider attending a couples' retreat or workshop together to deepen your connection and learn new skills for building intimacy.

Remember that building intimacy and connection takes time and effort, but the rewards can be immense. By prioritizing these activities in your relationship, you can build a stronger, more intimate bond with your partner.

Let us relax with a romantic poem before exploring the next chapter

A simple touch, a whispered word,
Our souls entwined, our hearts deferred,
In your embrace, I find my home,
With every kiss, my love has grown.

OUR BOND UNBREAKABLE, our passion fierce,
Our love an endless, boundless sphere,
Together we laugh, together we cry,
Our intimacy, our connection, never to die.

IN YOUR EYES, I SEE my soul,
Our love, an eternal, sacred goal,

Our hearts intertwined, forevermore,
Our intimacy and connection, an unbreakable core.

IN THE NEXT CHAPTER, we will explore the importance of commitment and dedication in relationships.

Chapter 11: The Importance of Commitment and Dedication

"Commitment and dedication are the promises we make to our loved ones, and the glue that binds us together through the ups and downs of life. They are the steady flame that keeps our love burning bright, and the anchor that keeps us grounded in a world of change. Let us never underestimate the power of commitment and dedication in our relationships."

COMMITMENT AND DEDICATION are two essential components of any long-lasting and fulfilling relationship. When couples are committed to each other and dedicated to making the relationship work, they are able to weather challenges and difficulties and emerge stronger and more connected.

Commitment involves making a conscious decision to stay committed to the relationship, even in the face of challenges and difficulties. This means being willing to work through conflicts and disagreements, and being willing to make compromises and sacrifices in order to strengthen the relationship.

Dedication involves being willing to put in the time and effort necessary to build a strong and healthy relationship. This means being willing to prioritize the relationship above other aspects of your life, and being willing to make the necessary investments in time, energy, and resources to keep the relationship strong.

There are several ways to build commitment and dedication in a relationship. The first is to be willing to communicate openly and honestly with your partner. This means being willing to share your thoughts and feelings, and being willing to listen to your partner's thoughts and feelings in return.

Another way to build commitment and dedication is to be willing to make compromises and sacrifices in order to meet your partner's needs. This means being willing to work together to find solutions that meet both partners' needs, even if those solutions require some sacrifices or compromises.

It is also important to be willing to make the necessary investments in time, energy, and resources to keep the relationship strong. This means setting aside time each week for quality time together, and being willing to make financial investments in the relationship if necessary.

Finally, it is important to be willing to work through conflicts and disagreements in a healthy and productive way. This means being willing to listen to each other's concerns and feelings, and being willing to work together to find solutions that meet both partners' needs.

Building commitment and dedication takes time and effort, but it is essential to building a strong and healthy relationship.

Activities for the Importance of Commitment and Dedication in Relationships:

1. Write down your personal values and discuss them with your partner. Make sure to include what you believe is important in a relationship, and how you plan to dedicate yourself to fulfilling those values.
2. Plan a date night once a week or bi-weekly where you both unplug from technology and spend quality time together, talking and reconnecting.
3. Create a relationship vision board together. Cut out pictures

and phrases from magazines or print images from the internet that represent what you want your relationship to look and feel like. Display it somewhere you both can see it regularly as a reminder of your commitment.

4. Take turns planning surprises for each other, whether it's a small gesture like leaving a love note, or a bigger surprise like planning a weekend getaway.

5. Make a list of your goals and aspirations as individuals and as a couple. Discuss how you can support each other in achieving those goals and hold each other accountable.

6. Practice forgiveness and work through conflicts together. Make a commitment to communicate openly and honestly, and find ways to compromise and move forward together.

7. Plan a project or activity that requires teamwork, such as a home improvement project or volunteering together for a cause you both care about. This can help strengthen your commitment to working together towards a common goal.

8. Make time for physical intimacy regularly. This can help deepen your connection and strengthen your commitment to each other.

9. Practice gratitude by regularly expressing appreciation for each other and the things you do together. This can help reinforce your dedication to your relationship.

10. Take time to reflect on your commitment to each other and your relationship. Discuss any challenges you're facing and work together to find solutions and strengthen your bond.

Let us relax with a romantic poem before exploring the next chapter

In love, there's a promise we make,
To stay together, no matter what it takes?
We pledge to be there, through thick and thin,
Our commitment to each other never grows thin.

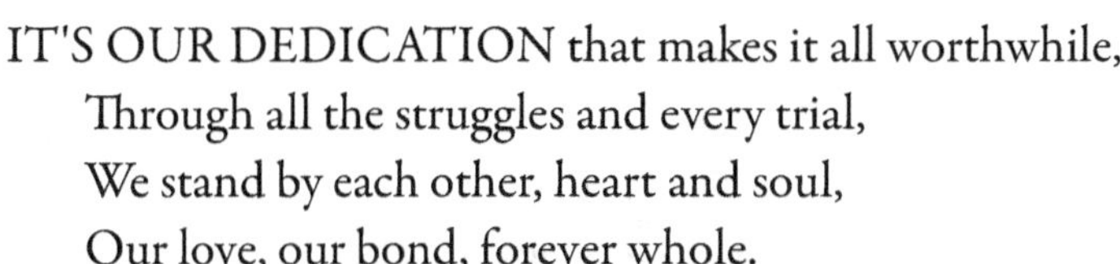

IT'S OUR DEDICATION that makes it all worthwhile,
Through all the struggles and every trial,
We stand by each other, heart and soul,
Our love, our bond, forever whole.

IN THIS COMMITMENT, we find our strength,
Through the ups and downs, we go to great lengths,
Our love, a flame that never fades,
For each other, we'll always serenade.

IN THE NEXT CHAPTER, we will explore the importance of trust and respect in relationships.

Chapter 12: The Importance of Trust and Respect

"Trust and respect are the foundations on which strong and healthy relationships are built. Without them, we are merely ships adrift in a sea of uncertainty and doubt. Let us cherish and nurture these virtues, for they are the beacons that guide us towards a love that endures."

Wouldn't you like to explore more with an interesting love story that sets the unparallel example of the importance of trust and respect?

IF YES THEN ENJOY IT-

Badal was a talented mathematician who lived in a small village in Ramnagar West Champaran. He spent most of his days teaching young minds in the local school. Reshma, on the other hand, was a foundation building expert for little learners in a prestigious school in New Delhi.

Despite the vast differences in their upbringing, they met by chance at a national education conference. They were both passionate about teaching and soon discovered they had a lot in common. They talked for hours about their work and soon realized that they had a strong connection.

Badal was from a poor family and had never been to the city. Reshma, on the other hand, was a city girl who had never experienced life in a village. Despite their differences, they continued to talk and learn more about each other. Over time, they fell in love.

As their relationship progressed, they faced many challenges. They struggled to communicate effectively due to their different languages and cultures. However, they never gave up on each other. They worked hard to understand and respect each other's differences, which ultimately strengthened their bond.

One day, Badal decided to take a big step and visit Reshma in New Delhi. He was nervous and excited to see her in her own environment. Reshma showed him around the city and introduced him to her family and friends. Badal was amazed at the modern lifestyle in the city, but he also missed the simplicity of his village.

During his visit, they realized that trust and respect were the keys to sustaining their relationship. They promised to always communicate openly and honestly, and to never judge each other based on their backgrounds or beliefs. They knew that their love was strong enough to overcome any obstacle.

After a year of dating, Badal proposed to Reshma and she said yes. They decided to get married in a traditional ceremony that combined both of their cultures. It was a beautiful celebration that brought together their families and friends.

From that day on, Badal and Reshma continued to learn from each other and grow together. They proved that true love can transcend boundaries and that trust and respect are essential for a healthy and lasting relationship.

Now come to the point again

Trust and respect are two essential components of any healthy and fulfilling relationship. When couples trust and respect each other, they are able to build a strong foundation of mutual understanding and support.

Trust involves being able to rely on your partner and feel secure in the relationship. This means being able to trust that your partner will be honest and loyal, and being able to trust that your partner will be there for you in good times and bad.

Respect involves valuing your partner as a person and treating them with dignity and consideration. This means being willing to listen to your partner's thoughts and feelings, and being willing to consider their perspective when making decisions that affect the relationship.

Building trust and respect in a relationship takes time and effort, but it is essential to building a strong and healthy relationship. There are several ways to build trust and respect in a relationship.

The first is to be open and honest with your partner. This means being willing to share your thoughts and feelings, even if they are difficult or uncomfortable to talk about. It also means being willing to be vulnerable and share your insecurities and fears.

Another way to build trust and respect is to be consistent in your words and actions. This means following through on your commitments, being reliable and dependable, and being consistent in the way you treat your partner.

It is also important to be willing to listen to your partner's perspective and show empathy and understanding. This means being willing to put yourself in their shoes and try to understand their point of view, even if you don't agree with it.

Finally, it is important to be willing to make the necessary investments in the relationship to keep it strong. This means setting aside time each week for quality time together, being willing to make compromises and sacrifices to meet each other's needs, and being willing to work through conflicts and disagreements in a healthy and productive way.

When couples build trust and respect in their relationship, they are able to build a strong and healthy foundation for their love to endure beyond time and space.

Activities that can help foster and reinforce the importance of respect in relationships:

1. **Use kind language:** Be mindful of the words you use when speaking to your partner. Using kind and respectful language

can help prevent misunderstandings and hurt feelings.

2. **Show appreciation:** Expressing gratitude for your partner's contributions and efforts can show respect and help maintain a positive dynamic in the relationship.

3. **Practice forgiveness:** Forgiveness is a key component of a respectful relationship. Practicing forgiveness can help prevent resentment and promote understanding.

4. **Set healthy boundaries:** Setting and respecting healthy boundaries is a way to show respect for each other's autonomy and individuality.

5. **Take an interest in each other's hobbies:** Showing an interest in your partner's hobbies and passions can help create a deeper bond and show respect for their interests.

6. **Practice empathy:** Putting yourself in your partner's shoes and trying to understand their perspective can help show respect and foster compassion in the relationship.

7. **Practice open and honest communication:** Communicating openly and honestly is a sign of respect for each other's feelings and creates a foundation of trust in the relationship.

8. **Celebrate differences:** Embracing each other's differences and unique qualities can help show respect for each other's individuality and promote a more positive dynamic in the relationship.

Let us relax with a romantic poem before exploring the next chapter

In the dance of love, trust is the beat,
The rhythm that makes our hearts complete,
Respect is the melody that weaves,
The harmony that our love retrieves.

OUR SOULS ARE BOUND by this sacred tie,
    A bond that only trust can amplify,
    Respectful words and deeds keep us aligned,
    A love so pure and rare, impossible to confine.

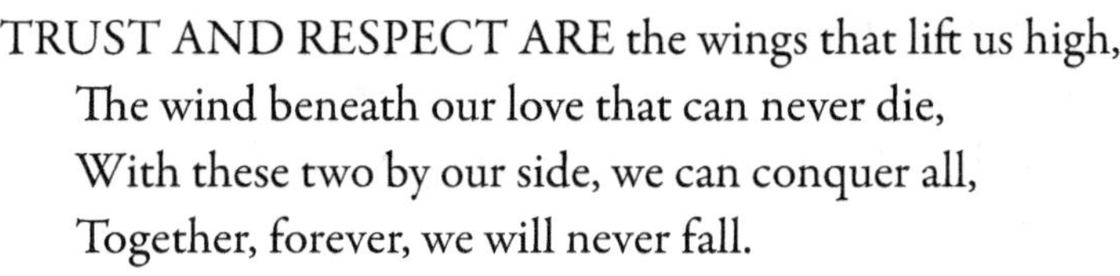

TRUST AND RESPECT ARE the wings that lift us high,
    The wind beneath our love that can never die,
    With these two by our side, we can conquer all,
    Together, forever, we will never fall.

IN THE NEXT CHAPTER, we will explore the importance of forgiveness in relationships.

Chapter 13: The Power of Forgiveness in Relationships

"Forgiveness is not a weakness, but a strength that can mend even the deepest wounds in a relationship. It is the key that unlocks the door to healing and growth, allowing us to move forward with love and understanding. Let us not forget the power of forgiveness in our journey towards a fulfilling and lasting relationship."

FORGIVENESS IS A POWERFUL tool for healing and strengthening relationships. It allows couples to move past hurt and pain and rebuild trust and respect in their relationship.

Forgiveness is not always easy, especially when we have been deeply hurt or betrayed by our partner. It can be difficult to let go of our anger and resentment and choose to forgive instead.

However, forgiveness is essential for a healthy and fulfilling relationship. When we hold onto grudges and refuse to forgive our partner, we create a toxic environment in our relationship that can ultimately lead to its demise.

Forgiveness involves letting go of our anger and resentment towards our partner and choosing to move forward in a positive and loving way. It does not mean forgetting or excusing our partner's behavior, but rather choosing to let go of the negative emotions associated with the hurt they caused.

One of the most important things to remember about forgiveness is that it is a process. It takes time and effort to work through our emotions and come to a place of forgiveness.

It is also important to communicate openly and honestly with our partner about our feelings and our willingness to forgive. This means being willing to listen to our partner's perspective and being open to the possibility of reconciliation.

Forgiveness is not always easy, but it is essential for a healthy and fulfilling relationship. When couples are able to forgive each other and move forward in a positive and loving way, they are able to build a strong and lasting foundation for their love to endure beyond time and space.

Activities for the Power of Forgiveness in Relationships:

1. **Write a forgiveness letter:** Sit down with your partner and write a letter to them forgiving them for any past hurts or mistakes. Encourage them to do the same for you. Then, exchange letters and read them aloud to each other.

2. **Practice empathy:** Take turns putting yourself in each other's shoes and sharing how you think the other person may have felt in a particular situation. This will help you both to understand each other's perspectives and foster forgiveness.

3. **Try a forgiveness meditation:** Find a quiet place to meditate and focus on forgiveness. Visualize yourself forgiving your partner and ask for forgiveness in return. This can help to release any negative emotions and promote healing in your relationship.

4. **Make a forgiveness jar:** Decorate a jar together and label it as your forgiveness jar. Whenever one of you feels hurt or upset by the other, write it down on a slip of paper and place it in the jar. Set a time each week to go through the slips of paper and forgive each other for any hurtful actions or words.

5. **Take responsibility:** Sometimes it's important to take responsibility for your own mistakes and apologize without

being prompted. This shows your partner that you are aware of your actions and are committed to making things right.

6. **Practice gratitude:** Take time each day to express gratitude for your partner and the positive aspects of your relationship. This can help to shift your focus away from negative emotions and towards forgiveness and appreciation.

7. **Seek counseling:** If forgiveness seems too difficult to achieve on your own, consider seeking the help of a professional counselor. A trained therapist can help guide you through the forgiveness process and help you both to heal and move forward.

Let us relax with a romantic poem before exploring the next chapter

In the journey of love, we make mistakes,
But forgiveness is the key that unlocks the gates,
It's the power that can heal the deepest wounds,
And bring love back to bloom.

FORGIVENESS IS NOT weakness, but strength,
To let go of grudges and find peace at length,
To understand, to empathize, and to mend,
And to find a love that's bound to transcend.

FOR LOVE WITHOUT FORGIVENESS is incomplete,
But with it, it's a story that's bittersweet,
A story of two hearts that beat as one,
Forged by the power of forgiveness, love, and fun.

IN THE NEXT CHAPTER, we will explore the importance of maintaining a healthy balance of independence and interdependence in relationships.

Chapter 14: The Importance of Independence and Interdependence

"In love, we must strive for the delicate balance of independence and interdependence. To stand strong on our own and yet willing to lean on each other when needed. Only then can we create a relationship that is both secure and free, both supportive and empowering."

MAINTAINING A HEALTHY balance of independence and interdependence is crucial in any relationship. While it is important to have a strong connection with our partner, it is equally important to maintain our own individuality and sense of self.

In order to achieve a healthy balance, both partners must be willing to respect and support each other's individual goals and aspirations. This means giving each other the space and freedom to pursue their own interests and hobbies, while also prioritizing time to spend together.

On the other hand, it is also important to foster a sense of interdependence in the relationship. This means recognizing that we are not independent entities, but rather two individuals who have chosen to come together as a couple.

Interdependence involves supporting each other emotionally, mentally, and physically, and working together as a team to overcome challenges and achieve shared goals. It requires a willingness to communicate openly and honestly, and to make compromises when necessary.

Maintaining a healthy balance of independence and interdependence can be challenging, but it is essential for the long-term success of any relationship. It allows both partners to grow and evolve as individuals, while also strengthening their connection and love for each other.

When couples are able to find this balance, they are able to create a relationship that endures beyond time and space. They are able to weather any storm and overcome any obstacle, because they have a strong foundation of love and respect that is rooted in both their independence and their interdependence.

Activities for the importance of independence and interdependence in relationships:

1. Take turns planning a solo activity and a shared activity each week. This allows each person to pursue their individual interests while also making time for the relationship.

2. Practice active listening when discussing decisions that affect both partners. This involves hearing and respecting each other's perspectives without interrupting or dismissing them.

3. Set healthy boundaries and respect each other's space. It's important to have time to yourself to recharge and pursue your own interests.

4. Try a new activity together that neither of you have done before. This can create a sense of shared adventure and help you both explore new interests.

5. Identify areas where you can support each other's goals and dreams. Encourage each other to pursue personal growth and be each other's cheerleader.

6. Schedule regular check-ins to discuss how you can support each other's independence while also staying connected as a couple.

7. Celebrate each other's successes and accomplishments, both individually and as a couple. This reinforces the importance of both independence and interdependence in a healthy relationship.

8. Attend a workshop or seminar focused on the topic of independence and interdependence in relationships. This can provide new insights and tools for maintaining a healthy balance in your relationship.

LET US RELAX WITH A romantic poem before exploring the next chapter

Independence and interdependence, a delicate dance
In love, we strive for both, a perfect balance
To stand strong on our own, yet intertwined
A bond of trust, where hearts and souls align

WE GIVE EACH OTHER space to grow and explore
While cherishing the moments we have, and more
Together we rise, with a shared vision and goal
Individuality embraced, while love makes us whole

SO LET US DANCE THIS dance, with grace and ease
And revel in the beauty of our interwoven destinies
For in each other, we find the strength to soar
A love that endures, forever more.

IN THE FINAL CHAPTER, we will explore how couples can continue to nurture their love and connection over time, and how they can ensure that their relationship continues to endure for years to come.

Chapter 15: Nurturing Love and Connection over Time

Maintaining a long-lasting, loving relationship requires ongoing effort and attention. It is not enough to simply find the right person and hope for the best; we must actively work to nurture and strengthen our love and connection over time.

Let us understand the secret facts with an example love story of Reshma and Badal.

Badal and Reshma had been together for several years now, and their love had only grown stronger with time. They had faced many challenges along the way, but they had always managed to overcome them together.

As they sat on their balcony, watching the sunset, Badal put his arm around Reshma and said, "I love you more every day."

Reshma smiled and leaned her head on his shoulder. "I love you too, Badal. I feel so lucky to have you in my life."

Badal and Reshma had learned that the key to a successful relationship was to always put each other first. They made time for each other every day, no matter how busy their schedules were. They listened to each other's needs and respected each other's boundaries.

But they also knew that it wasn't enough to just focus on the present. They wanted to ensure that their relationship continued to endure for years to come.

One day, Badal surprised Reshma with a romantic dinner on the beach. As they sat under the stars, Badal said, "Reshma, I want to spend the rest of my life with you. Will you marry me?"

Tears welled up in Reshma's eyes as she said yes. They had always talked about getting married, but this moment made it feel more real than ever before.

As they started planning their wedding, they also talked about their future together. They discussed their dreams and goals, and how they could support each other in achieving them. They knew that their love was strong enough to weather any storm, but they also wanted to be proactive in nurturing their connection.

They decided to start a new tradition: every year on their anniversary, they would take a trip together and reflect on their relationship. They would talk about what they had learned, what they wanted to improve, and what they were grateful for.

Years went by, and Badal and Reshma's love continued to flourish. They had their ups and downs, but they always worked through them with love and respect. They raised a family together, and their children learned from their example how to love and care for another person.

As they sat on their balcony, watching their grandchildren play in the garden, Badal turned to Reshma and said, "We've had an amazing life together. I'm so glad we took the time to nurture our love and connection."

Reshma smiled and squeezed his hand. "Yes I do love too, Badal."

I can't imagine my life without you. You're my forever."

So it is clear that

One of the most important ways to nurture love and connection is to prioritize quality time together. This means making a conscious effort to set aside distractions and focus solely on each other. It may mean scheduling date nights, taking a weekend getaway, or simply spending an evening at home with no other distractions.

Another important aspect of nurturing love and connection is to continue to grow and evolve as individuals, while also growing together as a couple. This means being open to new experiences and challenges, and supporting each other in pursuing personal growth and development.

Communication is also key in nurturing love and connection over time. It is important to be open and honest with each other, even when it is difficult. This means being willing to have difficult conversations and work through disagreements in a respectful and constructive manner.

Finally, it is important to remember to express love and appreciation for each other regularly. This can be done through words, actions, or small gestures of kindness. When we feel loved and appreciated, we are more likely to reciprocate those feelings and maintain a strong, loving connection with our partner.

Activities for nurturing love and connection over time in a relationship:

1. **Take a trip down memory lane:** Look through old photos or watch home videos together, reminiscing on past memories and milestones in your relationship.
2. **Try new things together:** Pick up a new hobby or activity that you both enjoy but haven't tried before, such as cooking a new type of cuisine, learning a new language, or taking dance lessons.
3. **Have date nights:** Set aside a designated night each week to have a date night, whether it's going out to dinner or trying a new activity together. It's important to prioritize quality time together and keep the romance alive.
4. **Volunteer together:** Find a cause that you're both passionate about and volunteer your time together to make a positive impact in your community.
5. **Create traditions:** Start creating meaningful traditions that you can continue to do together year after year, such as a

special holiday tradition or a weekly game night.

6. **Prioritize self-care:** Remember to prioritize self-care and encourage your partner to do the same. This will not only benefit your individual well-being, but also your relationship as a whole.

Let us relax with a romantic poem before exploring the next chapter

As time goes on, our love grows strong
Like a flower blooming all year long
We nurture our bond, day by day
And in each other's arms we'll always stay

OUR LOVE IS LIKE A tree, rooted deep
Growing stronger with each new leap
We weather storms and sunny days
Together we'll always find our way

WITH EACH PASSING YEAR, we grow old
But our love remains steadfast and bold
Nurturing our love is a labor of love
A gift we'll cherish from up above

IN THE END, NURTURING love and connection over time requires a willingness to put in the effort and prioritize the relationship above all else. When we are committed to our partner and to the growth and success of our relationship, we can create a love that endures beyond time and space.

Conclusion

In this book, we have explored the many dimensions of love and relationships, and how they can endure beyond time and space. From the importance of self-love and self-care, to the role of communication and compromise in healthy relationships, to the balance of independence and interdependence, and the ongoing effort required to nurture love and connection over time, we have seen how love can endure even in the face of great challenges.

But beyond all of the advice and guidance, the most important lesson we can take away from this book is that love is a choice.

It is a choice we make every day, to show up for our partner, to support them, to be there for them in both the good times and the bad. And when we make that choice, when we commit ourselves fully to the relationship, we can create a love that endures beyond time and space.

So it is the time to take a break but enjoy a romantic poem to relax long.

In the dimensions of love and relationships,
We find a world of endless connections.
A bond that grows with each passing day,
A love that weaves a beautiful collection.

LOVE IS NOT JUST A feeling in the heart,
But a reflection of our deepest desires.
It's a bond that we choose to embrace,

A commitment that sets our souls on fire.

IT'S IN THE LITTLE things we do each day,
The gentle touch, the smile we share.
It's in the moments of pure bliss,
The memories we create with care.

LOVE HAS MANY DIMENSIONS, it's true,
From friendship to passion, it can vary.
But at its core, it's a force that unites,
Bringing hearts together, never to vary.

THROUGH THE UPS AND downs of life,
Love remains a steadfast companion.
A source of strength and hope,
That keeps us moving forward, never undone.

SO LET US CHERISH THE dimensions of love,
And embrace the beauty of relationships.
For in the depth of our hearts,
We find a love that forever equips.

Don't miss out!

Visit the website below and you can sign up to receive emails whenever Rajesh Giri publishes a new book. There's no charge and no obligation.

https://books2read.com/r/B-A-OWRS-ISAGC

BOOKS 2 READ

Connecting independent readers to independent writers.

Did you love *Beyond Time and Space: A Love That Endures*? Then you should read *Scamming in the Shoe Market: An Inside Look*[1] by Rajesh Giri!

[2]

Are you tired of being scammed in the shoe market of Inderlok, Delhi?

Look no further!

This comprehensive guide offers invaluable insight into the fraudulent tactics used by scammers in this market and provides practical tips to help you protect yourself.

Learn about common scams and tricks used by these scammers to sell counterfeit products and rob unsuspecting customers of their hard-earned money.Discover effective ways to identify fake products and avoid becoming a victim of these unscrupulous individuals.Gain an

1. https://books2read.com/u/m2QB1G

2. https://books2read.com/u/m2QB1G

understanding of the consumer protection laws and market regulations in place to safeguard your interests as a shopper.Get shopping tips from experienced locals who know how to navigate the market and spot the difference between genuine and fake products.Whether you're a tourist or a local, this book is an essential resource for anyone looking to shop smart and stay safe in the shoe market of Inderlok, Delhi.

Don't let scammers take advantage of you! With the information and strategies presented in this book, you can become a savvy shopper and protect yourself against fraudulent practices in the shoe market of Inderlok, Delhi.

Also by Rajesh Giri

Scamming in the Shoe Market: An Inside Look
Still In Love With Her: A Guide To Sustain in a Long-Term
Relationship
Beyond Time and Space: A Love That Endures

About the Author

Rajesh Kumar Giri is a renowned lecturer of Mathematics, content writer, and a Practical Success Coach. With a passion for writing academic and educational content, Rajesh guides and trains people worldwide, breaking the barriers of language and region with his simple and easy-to-understand writing skills.

Rajesh's journey began in a poor family in a remote area of West Champaran, where he faced numerous challenges in paying for higher education. Despite the obstacles, he persevered and completed his degree, taking his first steps towards educating people and sharing his rags-to-riches ideas. Today, he resides in New Delhi, the capital of India, with his beautiful wife and two lovely sons, and he remains dedicated to serving poor students by providing free education online and offline.

Rajesh has been writing content in the education, affiliate marketing, and health niches since 2006. He believes that experiences speak louder than imaginary and bookish ideas, and his words connect with readers and result in conversions. As a Practical Success Coach, he helps people overcome their limiting beliefs and achieve their goals through practical techniques and strategies.

With his wealth of experience and passion for writing, Rajesh is committed to helping people around the world unlock their full potential and achieve success in all areas of their lives.

www.ingramcontent.com/pod-product-compliance
Lightning Source LLC
Chambersburg PA
CBHW052220150726
48002CB00003B/1206